EXTREME PREDATORS

John Allan

Picture Credits
(abbreviations: t = top; b = bottom; m = middle; l = left; r = right; bg = background)

Shutterstock: 16-17bg, 9ml; Alexander Wong 55br; Allesandro De Maddalena 1ml, 57mr, 76-77bg; Apiguide 7mr; Catmando 9bl, 18-19bg, 4-5bg; Clayton Harrison 1bm, 56br, 68-69bg; Colin Edwards Wildside 78tl; Daniel Eskridge 1br, 8tl, 9tl, 10-11bg, 12-13bg, 31tr; DenisaPro 79ml; Dirk Ercken 32tr, 36-37bg; Divespin.com 32bl, 42-43bg; Dotted Yeti 31ml; Edwin Butter 56bl, 62-63bg; Elenarts 9mr, 22-23bg; Eric Isselee 4-5bg; Fon Duangkamon 33br, 52-53bg; G images.com 33bl, 46-47bg; Herschel Hoffmeyer 8bl, 26-27bg, 31br (dinosaur); Imran Ashraf 1tr, 57ml, 57-58bg; JatPierstorff 56br, 60-61bg; Jayaprasanna T.L 57tr, 66-67bg; JENG BO YUAN 55tr; John Kasawa 4-5bg; Kaschibo 33tr, 40-41bg; Kessler Bowman 55ml; Kostiantyn Ivanyshen 9tr, 24-25bg, 30tr (landscape), 31br (landscape); Kshitij30 57tl, 64-65bg; Lukas Uher 8br, 20-21bg; Matis75 30tr (dinosaur); Michael Lynch 79tr; Milan Zygmunt 54bl; Ondrej Chvatal 56tl, 58-59bg; Pitiya Phinjongsakundit 33ml, 50-51bg; Protasov AN 1mr, 32br, 44-45bg; R Raymoonds 33mr, 48-49bg; RobJ808 54tr; Rodos Studio FERHAT CINAR 7tl, 9br, 28-29bg, 30bl; Shaftinaction 1m, 33tl, 38-39bg; Simongee 1tm, 6bl, 32tl, 34-35bg; SteffenTravel 1bl, 2tr, 57br, 72-73bg; Torook 78br; Tory Kallman 57bl, 74-75bg; Vladmir Turkenich 79br; Warpaint 1tl, 8, tr, 14-15bg.

Every effort has been made to trace the copyright holders and we apologize in advance for any unintentional omissions. We would be pleased to insert the appropriate credit in any subsequent edition of this publication.

First published in 2024
by Hungry Tomato Ltd
F15, Old Bakery Studios, Blewetts Wharf, Malpas Road,
Truro, Cornwall, TR1 1QH, UK

Thanks to our creative team
Senior Graphic Designer: Amy Harvey
Editor: Millie Burdett
Editor: Holly Thornton

Beetle Books is an imprint of Hungry Tomato

ISBN 9781916598614

Printed and bound in China

Discover more at:

www.mybeetlebooks.com
www.hungrytomato.com

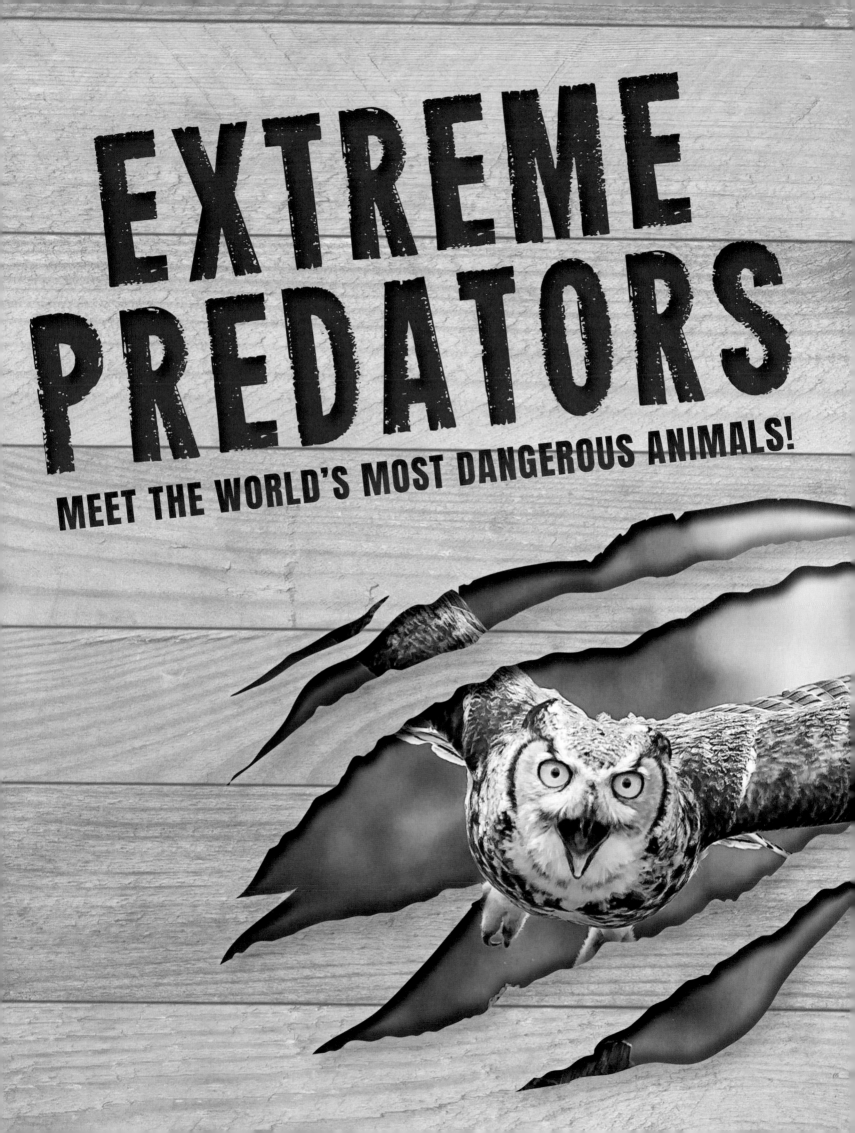

EXTREME PREDATORS

MEET THE WORLD'S MOST DANGEROUS ANIMALS!

CONTENTS

Words in **BOLD** can be found in the glossary

EXTREME PREDATORS

Which animal wins the title of the deadliest of all time?
This big question isn't as easy to answer as you might think...

THE DANGEROUS AND DEADLY

To help you make up your own mind, we have captured the most dangerous animals on Earth within the pages of this book!

FROM TINY TO GIGANTIC

The deadliest animals come in all shapes and sizes. Explore the top ten deadly animals in each category, from huge dinosaurs to small (but vicious!) piranhas...

ON THE MENU

Carnivores are animals that only eat meat, **herbivores** are animals that only eat plants and **omnivores** are animals that eat both! Most of the extreme **predators** we explore in this book are carnivores, which makes them the most dangerous of all!

DEADLY SCORES

Each animal has been rated based on how deadly they really are and put in order, counting down from least deadly to the most deadly! Which predators do you think will come out on top?

WARNING

THINGS GET GRIM FROM HERE ON IN... TURN THE PAGES TO FIND OUT MORE!

DEADLY DINOSAURS

Look at all of these prehistoric hunters; which one do you think is the ultimate extreme predator? Keep reading to find out...

DILOPHOSAURUS
This dino hunted in packs so that it could attack animals much larger than itself.

GIGANOTOSAURUS
Giganotosaurus is one of the largest carnivores that ever walked the Earth!

TYRANNOSAURUS REX
This dinosaur had massive jaws that could bite through even the biggest of bones!

ALBERTOSAURUS
This dinosaur's large size and fast speed made it a deadly hunter.

VELOCIRAPTOR

Velociraptors were fast-running dinosaurs, reaching speeds of up to 40 mph (65 km/h)!

SPINOSAURUS

This dinosaur had a tall **crest** along its back that was made of long, sharp spines!

TROODON

A Troodon typically had 120 curved teeth, perfect for slicing through flesh.

ALLOSAURUS

This dinosaur would attack plant-eating dinosaurs, as well as other predators, too!

CARCHARODONTOSAURUS

These large dinosaurs often picked fights with dinosaurs bigger than themselves!

DEINONYCHUS

Just one of these dinosaurs was scary enough, but no animal stood a chance against a whole pack!

DILOPHOSAURUS

Dilophosaurus lived during the early part of the **Jurassic** period. This carnivore had two bony ridges along the top of its skull that scientists believe was used for communication. The **fossil** remains of Dilophosaurus were discovered in 1942 in Arizona, USA.

CLEVER HUNTERS

Most scientists believe that Dilophosaurus hunted in packs, so it could attack animals much larger than itself. Dilophosaurus hunted by chasing its **prey**. Powerful muscles in its back legs meant it could run quickly.

DEADLY PREDATOR

Although Dilophosaurus' jaws were packed with long, sharp teeth, they were quite weak! Its claws, however, were very sharp and very deadly! It had a slender build, and an unusually long tail for an active predator.

DEADLY SCORE

WEIGHT
880 lbs
(400 kg)

DIET
Carnivore

LOCATION
North America

LETHAL POWERS
Sharp claws, powerful back legs and fast runner.

DEADLY COUNTDOWN

NO.10

VELOCIRAPTOR

Velociraptor was a feathered dinosaur that lived in Asia toward the end of the Cretaceous period. It had a powerful combination of speed, aggression and fearsome features – its small size is the only thing that stops it from being higher up on the deadly countdown!

SPEEDY THIEF

The name Velociraptor means "speedy thief". Despite being one of the most ferocious dinosaurs to date, they were only 6.5 feet (2m) long! One velociraptor may not seem too deadly, but a pack of them definitely would have been!

DEADLY SCORE

WEIGHT
up to 100 lbs
(45 kg)

DIET
Carnivore

LOCATION
Asia

LETHAL POWERS
Long claws, 80 razor sharp
teeth and fast runner.

SUPER SPEED
Velociraptors were fast-running
dinosaurs, reaching speeds of up to
40 mph (65 km/h). They hunted in
packs, often jumping onto the back of
their prey using their sharp claws to
hold on! A velociraptor typically had 80
teeth, designed for ripping and tearing
flesh easily.

DEADLY
COUNTDOWN
NO.9

GIGANUTUSAURUS

Giganotosaurus is one of the largest carnivores that ever walked the Earth. It is also one of the most mysterious of the meat-eating dinosaurs because it wasn't discovered until 1993.

THE GIANT

Giganotosaurus hunted by charging at its prey with its jaws wide open... scary! They attacked large herbivores using this technique, sometimes reaching speeds of 15 mph (24 km/h) – that's quick for such a big dinosaur!

DEADLY BUT DUMB

Giganotosaurus had jaws crammed with sharp, pointed teeth. They also had long tails that would have helped them stay balanced and turn quickly when running. They were fierce creatures, but despite being large in size, they had very small brains!

DEADLY SCORE

WEIGHT
up to 18,000 lbs
(8,120 kg)

DIET
Carnivore

LOCATION
South America

LETHAL POWERS
Large sharp teeth, fast runner and giant in size.

DEADLY COUNTDOWN
NO.8

TROODON

Troodon was a small dinosaur that lived during the Cretaceous period. The first Troodon fossil was discovered in 1855 in North America. Despite being small, it may have been the brainiest animal on Earth at the time.

OSTRICH OR TROODON?

In terms of body shape, the Troodon was similar to an ostrich! It had long legs and a light body weight which meant it could run very quickly. It is believed that it was covered in feathers, too.

EXCELLENT EYES

Troodons typically had 120 curved teeth, perfect for slicing through flesh. They also had large eyes that gave them excellent binocular vision, helping them spot and chase small **mammals**, lizards and snakes. It also meant they could hunt in the dark, allowing them to pounce on unsuspecting prey!

DEADLY SCORE

WEIGHT
up to 110 lbs
(50 kg)

DIET
Omnivore

LOCATION
Asia and
North America

LETHAL POWERS
Fast runner, super night vision
and curved sharp teeth.

DEADLY
COUNTDOWN

NO.7

CARCHARODONTOSAURUS

During the middle part of the Cretaceous period, this dinosaur was the top predator in North Africa. They were one of the largest dinosaurs and often picked fights with dinosaurs bigger than themselves. The first Carcharodontosaurus fossil was found in 1927 in Algeria, Africa.

SNEAKY HUNTERS

It is believed that a Carcharodontosaurus was a stealthy hunter, hiding and waiting until it could launch a surprise attack on its prey. It had sharp teeth and wide, powerful jaws that were the size of a human!

DEADLY SCORE

WEIGHT
Up to 14,000lbs
(6,350kg)

DIET
Carnivore

LOCATION
North Africa

LETHAL POWERS
Powerful jaws, sharp teeth and giant in size.

SLOW BUT POWERFUL

Carcharodontosaurus were big and fierce to look at, but they were also very slow movers. They relied on their power and weight to hunt, rather than speed. If the prey spotted a Carcharodontosaurus in time, they would probably be able to outrun it!

DEADLY COUNTDOWN

NO.6

ALBERTOSAURUS

Albertosaurus was a slim, saw-toothed predator that hunted large plant-eating dinosaurs. It lived in North America toward the end of the Cretaceous period. The first Albertosaurus fossil was found in 1884 in Canada.

MYSTERIOUS HUNTERS

Albertosaurus had a big head, with large, powerful jaws that were filled with around 60 razor-sharp teeth. Their eyes were positioned on the side of their head, which may have made it difficult for them to hunt, as predators see better when their eyes are at the front.

DEADLY SCORE

WEIGHT
5,500 lbs
(2,500kg)

DIET
Carnivore

LOCATION
North America

LETHAL POWERS
Powerful jaws, fast runner
and sharp teeth.

DEADLY COUNTDOWN

NO.5

DEADLY AND SCARY
This was still a very scary dinosaur!
Its large size and fast speed made
it a deadly hunter. It's believed the
Albertosaurus could run as fast as
19 mph (30 km/h), which is very quick
for a dinosaur of that size!

ALLOSAURUS

Allosaurus was one of the largest predators on Earth. It lived between the end of the Jurassic period and the beginning of the Cretaceous period. The first Allosaurus fossil was found in 1877 in North America.

TOP PREDATOR

Allosaurus was a predator with no natural enemies. It may have hunted in packs, using the large claws on its forelimbs to grab prey. This dinosaur would attack plant-eating dinosaurs as well as other predators, too!

DEADLY SCORE

WEIGHT
Up to 6,000 lbs
(2,700 kg)

DIET
Carnivore

LOCATION
Africa, Europe and
North America

LETHAL POWERS
Large claws, sharp teeth
and a fierce fighter.

DEADLY COUNTDOWN

NO.4

FIERCE OR FAKE?
They had sharp, long teeth. However,
they were fragile and broke off easily.
An Allosaurus could reach speeds of
up to 12 mph (19 km/h), but it had no
stamina for a long chase.

SPINOSAURUS

Spinosaurus was a fierce predator that lived during the Cretaceous period. It had a strange, tall crest along its back that was made of long spines. The first Spinosaurus fossil was discovered in Egypt in 1912.

LARGE CREST

The Spinosaurus had a slim body and long forelimbs, meaning it may have walked on all fours some of the time. Scientists think that the crest on its back was used to help it control its body temperature.

DEADLY SCORE

WEIGHT
Up to 38,000 lbs
(17,000 kg)

DIET
Carnivore

LOCATION
Africa

LETHAL POWERS
Narrow, snapping
jaws, heavy weight
and sharp teeth.

DEADLY COUNTDOWN

NO.3

FISH SNATCHER
This dinosaur had a long, narrow
jaw, just like a crocodile! The shape
of its jaws and teeth suggests that
Spinosaurus fed mainly on fish from
rivers and lakes.

TYRANNOSAURUS REX

This is the most famous of all the dinosaurs and one of the biggest land predators that has ever lived! It is often known as T. rex because "rex" means "king" in Latin. The first fossil was discovered in 1905.

TERRIFIC TEETH

This fierce dinosaur was extremely scary! It would probably have charged at its prey with its mouth wide open, showing off its impressive set of teeth. It could tear off huge chunks of flesh with a single bite!

DEADLY SCORE

WEIGHT
Up to 15,000 lbs
(7,000 kg)

DIET
Carnivore

LOCATION
Asia and
North America

LETHAL POWERS
Strong muscles, sharp teeth
and powerful jaws.

DEADLY COUNTDOWN

NO.2

SUPER SENSES

Tyrannosaurus had massive jaws with very powerful muscles that could bite through even the biggest of bones! They were very effective predators, thanks to their great sense of smell and forward-facing eyes. Tyrannosaurus probably stalked lots of plant-eating dinosaurs and picked off the weakest members.

DEINONYCHUS

It's less well-known than T. rex, but Deinonychus was the supreme dinosaur predator. It lived in North America during the early part of the Cretaceous period. The first Deinonychus fossil was found in 1931.

KNIFE-LIKE TEETH

Deinonychus had powerful jaw muscles and curved teeth. Each tooth could cut through skin and muscle like the blade of a knife! Because it was so small and light, Deinonychus was a very **agile** and fast-running predator. It could easily chase down dinosaurs much larger than itself!

DEADLY SCORE

WEIGHT
Up to 220 lbs (100 kg)

DIET
Carnivore

LOCATION
North America

LETHAL POWERS
High stamina, sharp curved teeth and strong limbs.

PACK HUNTERS

Just one of these dinosaurs was scary enough, but no animal stood a chance against a whole pack! Deinonychus hunted in large groups, often jumping on the back of their prey and tearing their flesh with both claws and teeth.

DEADLY COUNTDOWN

NO.1

CLOSE, BUT NOT CLOSE ENOUGH!

The dinosaurs below were all extreme predators but didn't quite make the top ten list! Which do you think looks the deadliest?

HERRERASAURUS

Herrerasaurus was one of the very first meat-eating dinosaurs. It lived in South America during the **Triassic period**, millions of years before T. rex and Deinonychus. It walked and ran on its hind legs and would have hunted plant-eating dinosaurs.

COELOPHYSIS

Coelophysis was a vicious pack-hunter that lived in North America during the late Triassic period. It was extremely agile and looked similar to long-legged birds we now see today.

BARYONYX

Baryonyx was a slightly smaller relative of Spinosaurus that lived in Europe and Africa during the early Cretaceous period. Baryonyx was a **bipedal** dinosaur that probably hunted fish, snatching them out of the water with its long jaws.

COMPSOGNATHUS

Compsognathus was one of the smallest known dinosaurs, about the size of a chicken, and lived during the middle of the Jurassic period. Compsognathus used the claws on its front feet to hold its prey while it bit off chunks of flesh. Small but deadly!

STRUTHIOMIMUS

This fast, bipedal omnivore lived in North America during the late Cretaceous period. It had large eyes at the sides of its head, and was constantly on the alert for danger. When spotted by larger predators, Struthiomimus could run away at speeds of up to 40 mph (65 km/h).

LETHAL KILLERS

Look at all of these lethal killers, which one do you think is the ultimate extreme predator? Keep reading to find out...

PIRANHA

This fish has earned its nickname of the "Wolf of the Waters"!

POISON DART FROG

This small but deadly frog is covered in a **poisonous** slime.

STONEFISH

Meet the fish that looks just like a rock, but don't let its appearance trick you!

PALESTINE SCORPION

The Palestine scorpion is so deadly that local people have given it the name "Deathstalker".

FUNNEL-WEB SPIDER

The funnel-web spider is one of the most dangerous spiders on Earth.

BLUE-RINGED OCTOPUS

The blue-ringed octopus is the only octopus that has a **venomous** bite.

MOSQUITO

Mosquitoes may be small, but they are lethal killers – they drink human blood!

BEAKED SEA SNAKE

This one **species** is responsible for about half of all sea snake attacks.

FIERCE SNAKE

The fierce snake can strike faster than the eye can see.

SEA WASP JELLYFISH

When a sea wasp jellyfish **stings** its victims, it can stop their heart beating in just a few seconds!

PIRANHA

This fish has earned its nickname of the "Wolf of the Waters"! It has sharp teeth, hunts in groups and has a big appetite for meat. One piranha will give you a nasty bite, but a group of hungry piranhas could eat even larger animals!

ALIVE PREY

Piranhas are lethal predators. They don't kill their prey; they just start eating it alive!

SUPER SENSES

The piranha also has a super sense of smell and can detect blood in the water even if it's far away. It may not often attack humans, but it can still be deadly, so watch where you swim!

DEADLY SCORE

WEIGHT
17 lb
(8 kg)

DIET
Carnivore

LOCATION
South America

LETHAL POWERS
Super sense of smell, sharp teeth and very aggressive.

DEADLY COUNTDOWN

NO.10

POISON DART FROG

Most people think that small frogs are harmless, but the poison dart frog would prove them wrong! This frog lives in the tropical rainforests of Central and South America. Native people sometimes put the frog's poison on their arrows when they go hunting.

FIERCE DEFENDERS

Poison dart frogs use the poison they make to defend themselves from other predators. Their skin is covered in a poisonous slime, so just touching a poison dart frog can kill prey, no matter the size!

DESTRUCTIVE DIET

This frog mainly feeds on insects, especially ants, which it needs to eat in order to produce its poison! This poison is then released from its glands, ready to kill its prey!

DEADLY SCORE

WEIGHT
Up to 0.02 lbs
(0.01 kg)

DIET
Carnivore

LOCATION
Central and
South America

LETHAL POWERS
Poisonous slime and
incredible agility.

DEADLY COUNTDOWN

NO.9

FUNNEL-WEB SPIDER

The funnel-web spider is one of the most dangerous spiders on Earth. Although it mainly lives in the woodland, the Sydney funnel-web spider can also be found in houses underneath floors, and in garages. This lethal killer lives in Sydney, Australia.

STICKY HUNTER

The Sydney funnel-web spider hunts by making a web and waiting for its prey to get stuck in it, before biting it and releasing its **venom** into the prey.

DEADLY SCORE

WEIGHT
Unknown

DIET
Carnivore

LOCATION
Australia

LETHAL POWERS
Deadly venom, agile and clever hunter.

DEADLY COUNTDOWN

NO.8

DEADLY VENOM

A funnel-web spider can kill prey in 15 minutes with just one bite. Unlike most other spiders, the funnel-web spider can be very deadly to humans as well as animals!

BLUE-RINGED OCTOPUS

The blue-ringed octopus is not only one of the most beautiful of all sea creatures – it's also one of the most deadly! This small, shy animal lives in the Indian and Pacific Oceans. Swimmers have learned not to go looking for it because it has a very nasty bite!

POWERFUL BITE

The blue-ringed octopus is the only octopus that has a venomous bite. Before killing it, the venom makes prey unable to move their body. What a nasty attack!

EASY PREY

This octopus mostly feeds on crabs and wounded fish that can't get away. It has a sharp beak that makes it easy to slice through flesh.

DEADLY SCORE

WEIGHT
Up to 0.18 lbs
(0.08 kg)

DIET
Carnivore

LOCATION
Indian and
Pacific Oceans

LETHAL POWERS
Quick, venomous bite
from a sharp beak.

DEADLY COUNTDOWN

NO.7

STONEFISH

Meet the fish that looks just like a rock! The stonefish lives around the coasts of the Indian and Pacific Oceans. Not only is it very unusual to look at, it's also extremely dangerous. The stonefish is the most venomous fish in the sea!

STONE OR FISH?

This predator is great at blending in! The stonefish has lumpy skin that acts as a natural **camouflage**. It changes its appearence to match the habitat its in. It's prey don't know its there!

SHARP ATTACK

The stonefish will lie close to the seabed to hide from unsuspecting prey. There, it will wait for its prey to swim by before using its spines to attack! Its sharp spines easily stab through flesh and contain deadly venom that can kill quickly.

DEADLY SCORE

WEIGHT
Up to 4 lbs (2 kg)

DIET
Carnivore

LOCATION
Indian and Pacific Oceans

LETHAL POWERS
Sharp spines, deadly venom and great camouflage skills.

DEADLY COUNTDOWN

NO.6

PALESTINE SCORPION

The Palestine scorpion is the most dangerous scorpion in the world! It's found in the deserts and scrubland of the Middle East and North Africa. The Palestine scorpion is so deadly that local people have given it the name "Deathstalker".

DANGEROUS PINCERS

The Palestine scorpion hunts insects but doesn't use its sting. instead, it tears its prey apart with its **pincers**!

VENOMOUS TAIL

Palestine scorpions only use their sharp tail to inject deadly venom when they feel threatened. The scorpion will often sting its victim over and over again!

DEADLY SCORE

WEIGHT
0.2 lbs
(0.09 kg)

DIET
Carnivore

LOCATION
Middle East and
North Africa

LETHAL POWERS
Strong pincers, sharp tail
and deadly venom.

DEADLY
COUNTDOWN

NO.5

FIERCE SNAKE

The fierce snake is not as famous as cobras and rattlesnakes, but it's much more dangerous! It has the deadliest venom of any snake on land. Luckily for its prey, the fierce snake is very rare!

SNEAKY HUNTER

Fierce snakes can strike faster than the eye can see! They mainly hunt small mammals, which they swallow whole. As they bite their victims, two fangs inject a small dose of venom. Prey normally dies within seconds.

REMAIN CALM

As well as being rare to find, the fierce snake is usually very shy. If you are unlucky enough to see one, walk slowly away, because they can be very aggressive if disturbed...

DEADLY SCORE

WEIGHT
Up to 4 lbs
(2 kg)

DIET
Carnivore

LOCATION
Australia

LETHAL POWERS
Sharp fangs, deadly venom and agile.

DEADLY COUNTDOWN

NO.4

BEAKED SEA SNAKE

This sea snake is a bad-tempered killer. The beaked sea snake lives in the waters surrounding the Philippines and North Australia. This one species is responsible for about half of all sea snake attacks! Its venom is deadlier than most other creatures on land.

LOOK OUT!

The vivid black markings on the beaked sea snake make it easy to identify. They have a special flat tail for swimming and thin skin over their nostrils which close when in water.

DEADLY SCORE

WEIGHT
Up to 3 lbs
(1.3 kg)

DIET
Carnivore

LOCATION
Philippines and
North Australia

LETHAL POWERS
Deadly venom, agile and
very aggressive.

DEADLY COUNTDOWN

NO.3

POISONOUS HUNTERS
These predators hunt by injecting
venom into the muscles and
stopping their prey from breathing.
The beaked sea snake can swallow
prey twice the size of its neck!

MOSQUITO

"Mosquito" means "little fly", but don't be fooled by their small size. Mosquitoes drink human blood! Some of these mosquitoes can pass on a deadly disease called **malaria**. This disease has killed more people than any other on our planet.

TASTY BLOOD

Female mosquitoes must drink blood in order to lay eggs. They are only interested in drinking the blood of mammals – humans are easy targets! Mosquito adults also feed on fruits for energy so they can fly for longer and find as much prey as possible!

FATAL SUCKERS

Mosquitoes do not have teeth. Instead, they have a feeding tube that looks like a sharp needle! They jab this into human skin to suck up blood. They only need to take a tiny drop of blood from each human for the results to be fatal!

DEADLY SCORE

WEIGHT
Just over 1 lb
(up to 5 milligrams)

DIET
Omnivore

LOCATION
Nearly everywhere!

LETHAL POWERS
Agile, sharp needle-like mouth and carries diseases.

DEADLY COUNTDOWN

NO.2

SEA WASP JELLYFISH

No living creature is more deadly than the Sea Wasp Jellyfish. It has dozens of stinging tentacles with a deadly venom that kills almost instantly. To make it worse, this jellyfish is transparent, meaning it's almost impossible to spot under water!

FREAKY FEATURES

The sea wasp jellyfish has a clear box-shaped body and can grow tentacles up to 10 feet (3m) long, perfect for reaching out to sting its victims! This type of jellyfish is also known for having extremely good eyesight. The jellyfish can spot danger from far away and can attack before it becomes the predator's meal.

DEADLIEST JELLYFISH

Each tentacle has sharp, sensitive points that inject deadly venom at the smallest of touches. When a sea wasp jellyfish stings its victims, it can stop their heart from beating in just a few seconds! To protect people, many beaches close when there are sea wasp jellyfish around.

DEADLY SCORE

WEIGHT
Up to 4 lbs (2 kg)

DIET
Carnivore

LOCATION
Australia

LETHAL POWERS
Hard to spot, deadly venom and stinging tentacles.

DEADLY COUNTDOWN

NO.1

CLOSE, BUT NOT CLOSE ENOUGH!

The animals below are all lethal killers but didn't quite make the top ten list! Which one do you think looks like the most lethal killer?

CONE SHELL

If you saw one of these on the beach, you might be tempted to pick it up – bad move! All cone shells can inflict a painful sting, with some also releasing deadly **toxins**.

GILA MONSTER

This strange-looking **reptile** is one of the few venomous lizards in the world. It has teeth that are covered in venom strong enough to kill an adult human!

STINGRAY

The stingray is closely related to sharks, but you don't have to worry about its bite – it's the sting in the tail that's the problem! This fish lives in shallow water; swimmers beware!

HARVESTER ANT

They may be little, but you want to get out of the way of harvester ants! They have a sharp sting that injects dangerous venom if they feel threatened.

WESTERN DIAMONDBACK RATTLESNAKE

This snake is known for its rattle tail, which helps to warn off any danger, and for good reason! This lethal killer bites fast and deep, injecting deadly venom into its victims.

FIERCE PREDATORS

Look at all of these fierce predators which one do you think is the ultimate extreme predator? Keep reading to find out...

LEOPARD
Powerful limb and neck muscles make the leopard the strongest climber of the big cats.

COYOTE
Coyotes are ruthless predators that hunt day and night.

POLAR BEAR
They are excellent swimmers, with their powerful muscles being the key to their deadly attack.

NILE CROCODILE
The Nile crocodile can bite but not chew, meaning it swallows its prey whole!

ROYAL BENGAL TIGER
They have excellent vision, seeing six times better than humans!

CHEETAH
The cheetah can run quicker than any other animal on Earth!

GREAT HORNED OWL
It is so deadly that it has earned the nickname "the tiger of the woods".

GREAT WHITE SHARK
They mostly eat seals, dolphins and other sharks, but will attack anything they think they can eat, including humans!

ORCA (KILLER WHALE)
Orcas often live and hunt in family groups and are known for their fierce hunting techniques.

AFRICAN LION
The African lion has five claws on each paw, perfect for grabbing onto and killing prey.

LEOPARD

The leopard is a secretive and deadly predator that only comes out at night! Powerful legs and neck muscles make it the strongest climber of the big cats. This big cat may sneak up on its prey through tall grass or wait on a tree branch before jumping down onto its victim!

STRONG HUNTERS
Unlike cheetahs (page 66) who rely on speed for hunting, these big cats rely on their strength. Leopards will often hunt and kill prey much larger than themselves!

CLEVER CAMOUFLAGE
Their spotted fur is perfect for camouflage, and their large paws contain very sharp claws for gripping onto prey.

DEADLY SCORE

WEIGHT
Up tp 212 lbs
(96 kg)

DIET
Carnivore

LOCATION
Asia and Africa

LETHAL POWERS
Powerful limbs, excellent
camouflage and sharp
curved claws.

DEADLY
COUNTDOWN
NO.10

COYOTE

A coyote is a type of wild dog, that has **adapted** to lots of different environments. No matter if it's snowy landscapes or desert plains, coyotes can thrive! They are ruthless predators that hunt day and night.

LONE HUNTERS

The coyote hunts alone, chasing prey over long distances without getting tired. They also have a great sense of smell that helps them sniff out prey hiding underground.

SHARP WEAPONS

Coyotes have sharp claws, but their teeth are their main weapons. They have 42 in total, all very strong and very sharp!

DEADLY SCORE

WEIGHT
Up to 45 lbs
(20 kg)

DIET
Carnivore

LOCATION
North America

LETHAL POWERS
Lots of sharp teeth,
excellent sense of smell
and high stamina.

DEADLY
COUNTDOWN

NO.9

POLAR BEAR

Polar bears are the largest and most powerful predators that live on land, and they have nothing to fear – except hunger! During warmer months, these huge creatures often go hungry because they can't hunt seals unless the sea is frozen. In these difficult times, a polar bear might not eat for months.

PATIENT HUNTERS

Polar bears will catch seals by waiting for them to come up to the surface. They use their sharp claws to easily rip through skin and muscle, and their tough jaws to crunch through bone.

SUPER SWIMMERS
Polar bears can swim constantly for days at a time, searching for prey!

DEADLY SCORE

WEIGHT
Up to 1,600 lbs
(725 kg)

DIET
Carnivore

LOCATION
Arctic

LETHAL POWERS
Powerful muscles, strong jaws and excellent swimmer.

DEADLY
COUNTDOWN
NO.8

RoYAL BENGAL TIGER

The Royal Bengal tiger is one of the largest of the big cats, second only to the Siberian tiger. Like all tigers, they are deadly predators and can develop an appetite for humans!

LETHAL HUNTERS
Royal Bengal tigers hunt by leaping onto their prey, dragging them down with sharp claws and biting their throats to kill them. They have the biggest teeth among the big cats, using them to take down animals larger than themselves.

EXCELLENT EYES
They have excellent vision, seeing six times better than humans!

DEADLY SCORE

WEIGHT
Up to 573 lbs
(260 kg)

DIET
Carnivore

LOCATION
Indian subcontinent

LETHAL POWERS
Excellent vision, fast runners
and large sharp teeth.

DEADLY
COUNTDOWN
NO.7

CHEETAH

The cheetah can run quicker than any other animal on Earth! It may be one of the smallest of the big cats, but it's also one of the deadliest. The cheetah uses its speed to catch fast-running prey on the grasslands of Africa.

SNEAKY HUNTERS

They hunt by creeping through long grass to get close to prey, before launching into a high-speed attack! The cheetah attacks with both teeth and claws all at once.

SPEEDY CATS

The cheetah has an unusually slim body, built for speed. Over short distances, it can reach a speed of nearly 60 mph (110 km/h).

DEADLY SCORE

WEIGHT
Up to 140 lbs
(64 kg)

DIET
Carnivore

LOCATION
Africa

LETHAL POWERS
Superfast runners, sharp teeth, stealthy hunters.

DEADLY COUNTDOWN
NO.6

NILE CROCODILE

The Nile crocodile is a cold-blooded killer but can be rather lazy when it comes to hunting. This large reptile prefers to lie in water, with only its eyes and nostrils showing, waiting for prey to come near enough to attack.

BIG HUNTERS

Like other reptiles, the Nile crocodile can bite but not chew. This means all of its prey is swallowed whole, no matter how big! This deadly predator can even take on giraffes! Long jaws full of sharp teeth are the Nile crocodile's main weapon.

DEADLY SCORE

WEIGHT
Up to 1,650lbs
(750kg)

DIET
Carnivore

LOCATION
Africa

LETHAL POWERS
Long jaws, sharp teeth and
very aggressive.

DEADLY COUNTDOWN

NO.5

SCALY SKIN
This fierce predator is covered in a
natural protective outer layer made of
bony plates that keeps it safe when
taking on big prey that might fight
back! The Nile crocodile travels fast
in the water but this beast can run
almost twice as quickly on land!

GREAT HORNED OWL

The great horned owl is an unusually deadly and dangerous predator, with the ability to kill prey up to three times its own size. It's so deadly that it has even earned the nickname "the tiger of the woods".

SUPER SKILLED

Great horned owls can't move their large eyes like humans can. Instead they have a very special skill. They can almost completely turn their neck around! This is a massive advantage when it comes to looking for prey.

STEALTHY HUNTERS

They mostly hunt at night, relying on their excellent sight and hearing. They dive down from high trees to snatch prey on the ground, flying and attacking without making any noise!

DEADLY SCORE

WEIGHT
Up to 4 lbs
(1.8 kg)

DIET
Carnivore

LOCATION
Africa

LETHAL POWERS
Silent flight, excellent senses and camouflaged feathers.

DEADLY COUNTDOWN
NO.4

AFRICAN LIuN

This lion is Africa's top predator, and for good reason! The females often communicate and hunt together to take down large animals, leaving the males to defend the **territory**. Lions are best known for their almighty roar!

FIERCE FEATURES

African lions have five claws on each paw, perfect for grabbing onto and killing prey. Their powerful jaws are packed with 30 sharp teeth, perfect for ripping flesh.

HERD HUNTING

When lions hunt, they help each other to make sure the prey is surrounded at all times, making sure it can't get away. That's deadly teamwork!

DEADLY SCORE

WEIGHT
Up to 420 lbs
(190 kg)

DIET
Carnivore

LOCATION
Africa

LETHAL POWERS
Hunt in groups, five claws per paw and sharp teeth.

DEADLY COUNTDOWN

NO.3

OrCA (KILLEr WHALE)

The orca deserves its popular nickname "killer whale". They are deadly top-predators with no natural enemies. Orcas often live and hunt in family groups, and are known for their fierce hunting techniques.

HUNGRY PREDATORS

An orca has up to 50 large pointed teeth but can't chew, so it has to swallow its prey whole, no matter the size.

CLEVER HUNTERS

They are very intelligent creatures, working together to find the best way to attack prey. Some use their tails to smack prey, others surround prey from all directions, and some even flip seals off icebergs!

DEADLY SCORE

WEIGHT
Up to 16,000 lbs
(7,260 kg)

DIET
Carnivore

LOCATION
Every ocean

LETHAL POWERS
Highly intelligent, large teeth and hunts in groups.

DEADLY COUNTDOWN NO.2

GREAT WHITE SHARK

The great white shark is the world's deadliest and most dangerous predator. This deadly killer mostly eats seals, dolphins and other sharks, but will attack anything it thinks it can eat, including humans!

SUPER SMELL
The great white shark has a fantastic sense of smell, helping it find wounded prey from far away.

TERRIFYING ATTACKER

This fierce predator attacks prey with a twisting lunge, tearing a chunk of flesh off, then waits for the victim to die before coming back to eat! Its rows of razor-sharp teeth slice through flesh easily, making it impossible for prey to escape once attacked.

DEADLY SCORE

WEIGHT
4,000 lbs
(1,814 kg)

DIET
Carnivore

LOCATION
Every ocean

LETHAL POWERS
Rows of sharp teeth, very aggressive and fantastic sense of smell.

DEADLY COUNTDOWN
NO.1

CLOSE, BUT NOT CLOSE ENOUGH!

The animals below are all fierce predators but didn't quite make the top ten list! Which one do you think looks the fiercest?

BALD EAGLE

The bald eagle is the national bird of the United States of America. The bald eagle loves to eat fish, often swooping down with its sharp talons to grab them straight out of the water!

TARANTULA

Tarantulas are the largest spiders in the world. Unlike other spiders, tarantulas don't spin webs. Instead, they're active hunters that prowl around at night looking for prey!

VAMPIRE BAT

This mammal has a fearsome reputation because of its diet – it feeds on the blood of other mammals! The vampire bat does not actually suck blood; it bites its victim then laps up the blood with its tongue.

WOLVERINE

The wolverine is the largest and fiercest member of the weasel family. It chases after small prey but will also climb trees to attack large prey from above!

PANGOLIN

The pangolin may not look fierce, but it's a mighty hunter. It uses its powerful claws to burrow into termite mounds and ant nests, and then uses its long tongue to slurp up their eggs. Its strange, hard, scale-covered coat protects the pangolin against ant bites and stings.

GLOSSARY

Adapt - able to fit in with surroundings.

Agile – able to move quickly and easily.

Ambush – when a predator hides and surprises others with an attack, unexpectedly.

Bipedal – having the ability to walk on two legs.

Camouflage – when an animal blends into its surroundings so it's hard to see.

Carnivores – meat-eating animals.

Crest – a ridge on the head of an animal.

Cretaceous period - a period in time between 145 and 66 million years ago.

Fossil – evidence of past life that has turned to stone over time.

Herbivore - plant-eating animals.

Herd – a group of animals of one kind that live or travel together.

Jurassic period - a period in time between 201 and 145 million years ago.

Malaria – an infectious disease transmitted to humans by the bite of an infected Anopheles mosquito.

Mammals – warm-blooded animals with a covering of hair on the skin and the ability to produce milk to feed their young.

Omnivores – animals that eat both meat and plants.

Pincers – the front claws of a lobster, crab, scorpion or similar creature.

Poison - a substance that can kill or hurt a person or animal.

Poisonous - something that contains or produces a substance that can kill or hurt a person or animal.

Predator – an animal that lives by attacking and killing other animals.

Prey – an animal hunted or caught for food.

Reptile – a cold-blooded animal that has scales and lays eggs on land.

Species – a group of living things that have the same features as each other and share a common name.

Stamina - lasting strength and energy.

Sting – a sharp, piercing part of an animal, often ejecting a venomous substance.

Territory - a specific area that belongs to or is controlled by someone or something.

Threatened - being in a situation where there is a risk or danger of harm, damage, or negative consequences.

Toxins - substances that can cause harm or injury to living organisms.

Triassic period - a period in time between 252 and 201 million years ago.

Venom – a poisonous substance of an animal, usually passed on by a bite or a sting.

Venomous – a creature that can produce venom (see above).

INDEX